HEALING YOURSELF

CHRISTIAN D. LARSON

Published by Left of Brain Books

Copyright © 2021 Left of Brain Books

ISBN 978-1-396-31742-2

First Edition

All rights reserved. No part of this publication may be reproduced, distributed, or transmitted in any form or by any means, including photocopying, recording, or other electronic or mechanical methods, without the prior written permission of the publisher, except in the case of brief quotations embodied in critical reviews and certain other noncommercial uses permitted by copyright law. Left of Brain Books is a division of Left of Brain Onboarding Pty Ltd.

Table of Contents

INTRODUCTORY STATEMENT	1
CHAPTER I. FULL SUPPLY OF VITAL ENERGY	2
CHAPTER II. THE SUPER-PHYSICAL BREATH	6
CHAPTER III. PSYCHOLOGICAL EQUILIBRIUM	11
CHAPTER IV. NOURISHING THE BODY	15
CHAPTER V. NOURISHING THE MIND	19
CHAPTER VI. THE WILL TO BE WELL	23
CHAPTER VII. INTERIOR RELAXATION	27
CHAPTER VIII. IMAGINE YOURSELF WELL	31
CHAPTER IX. THE REAL LIVING OF LIFE	35
CHAPTER X. THE RIGHT USE OF BODY, MIND AND SOUL	38
CHAPTER XI. THE FINER CURATIVE FORCES	46
CHAPTER XII. LIVING IN THE ABSOLUTE	54

INTRODUCTORY STATEMENT

There are many states and conditions of mind, and many stages in human development. Also, there are many special personal needs. Therefore, it is necessary to have many methods of healing and many ways to open the doors to personal emancipation and we being.

Upon the following pages many methods are presented, each one of which has proven its own efficacy and power in no uncertain manner; indeed, each one of these methods has helped its thousands, and will continue to do so.

The reader is advised, therefore, to study each chapter carefully so as to become thoroughly familiar with the place, the possibility and the application of each method, and selecting, for the present, those methods that make the deepest and most positive appeal.

Later, when needs arise for healing or physical and personal upbuilding, the best methods for the occasion will readily suggest themselves; and definite results may be secured in the least time with the least effort.

The larger purpose should be, however, to gain that wider consciousness through which we may combine, harmoniously, a worthy methods—the psychological, the metaphysical and the spiritual—causing a good things to work together for greater and greater good.

CHAPTER I.
FULL SUPPLY OF VITAL ENERGY

The Great Law.—It is absolutely impossible for any form of disease, physical or mental, organic or functional, to enter the human system so long as that system is abundantly supplied with vital energy. And it is absolutely impossible for any form of disease to remain in the human system after a full supply of vital energy has been provided for every part of that system.

The First Essential.—Recognizing the validity and the certainty of the law just presented, we realize that the first essential in the attainment of health, in the regaining of health, or in the maintenance of health, must necessarily be to supply the human system with a the vital energy that mind and body can appropriate and employ. In brief, if we have good health, and wish to continue in good health, we must take immediate steps to keep the system brim full of vital energy under every circumstance; or, if we wish to regain health, we must proceed to recharge and revitalize the entire system until the full supply of energy has been secured.

How to Proceed.—Our purpose must be, to so live, think and act that a waste of vital energy may be prevented absolutely; and also, to adopt such methods as may prove directly conducive to the increase of vital energy; that is, we must learn to retain what energy we have, and learn to produce more and more as growth and advancement may demand.

Practical Methods.—The first and simplest rule to observe is that of moderation in a things. Act only in conformity with present capacity; and aim to increase your capacity before you increase your activity. Believe that you can do as much as you like; then do only as much as you know you have the available energy to do at present. Take good care of the energy you have. Permit no waste; but do not permit the least to lie dormant. Use all the energy you have every day. Live and work to full capacity. But do not live and work beyond your present capacity. First, increase your capacity; and know that you can.

Revitalization.—When all the energy in the system has been used for the day, in wholesome living and constructive work, proper methods must be taken to revitalize and recharge the system. And this is accomplished in the natural way, through change of activity, recreation and sleep. Should you feel the energy of the system running low, the simplest and quickest way to recuperate is to go and do something else, or to turn thought and attention into some other channel. In brief, permit the muscles and the faculties you have been using to relax, and call into action muscles and faculties that have not been used for a time. The practice of turning thought and attention into other channels for thirty minutes several times every day is one of the best methods known for recharging the system with energy, and thus keeping mind and body fully supplied at a times.

Source of Energy.—The real source of vital energy is found in the subconscious mind; and we enter the subconscious whenever we go to sleep, largely for the purpose of gaining a new supply of life, force and energy. It is highly important, therefore, to go to sleep with the expectation of gaining a larger supply of energy than we ever possessed before, because it is always the law everywhere that the more we expect the more we receive. However, we must never permit anxiety to accompany our expectations; we must, in a things, be calm and serene, and make it our purpose to live and act in the full faith that all our expectations will be realized. The fact is, that there is more power in a calm, serene faith than in anything else in the world.

How to Live.—In order that the system may be full of life and energy at a times, live the serene life, but turn on the full current. Give full, harmonious and constructive expression to all the power there is in you, but see that every action is calm, orderly and in perfect poise. Live a large life and a powerful life, but invariably combine the expression of power with a deep feeling of peace. Try to feel serene and strong at the same time, and at a times. This is most important if you would have an abundance of energy, and retain it all with full force, in your own system. And you will find that this simple practice of trying to feel serene and strong at the same time will work wonders for you.

How to Work.—Under every circumstance, work in poise. Work with all the energy you have, but apply that energy in poise; and never permit yourself to violate this rule. Avoid nervous rush, regardless of conditions or demands; and also avoid the habit of doing less than you can do; for remember that we always lose what energy we do not use. Use all the energy you have; use it constructively; use it in poise; and use it in the full conviction that you will immediately receive more. Again, we should consider the great law of expectation. Expect more; expect much; expect everything you want; then live in the absolute faith that all your expectations will be realized.

Very Important.—All waste of energy must be prevented if we wish to have continuous and perfect health. And, therefore, everything must be avoided that may tend to produce such waste, be the action physical or mental. We must not only avoid the misuse of the body, but also the misuse of the mind. Such states therefore as anger, fear or worry, or similar states of mind must never be tolerated for a single moment. The fact is, that one hour of severe mental depression may lower your vital energy down to a point where you have less than one-fourth as much as you had before. If one hour of such a state of mind can destroy more than three-fourths of your energy, we have something here that must not be ignored for a moment. And it is too true that mental depression, or similar states, will have this very effect. We must therefore eliminate such states absolutely, and keep the mind in a clean, lofty, harmonious condition at a times. Remember this: *Do nothing to lower your vitality and you will always be well.*

Special Exercise.—We find in every human system a tendency to lose energy. In fact, most people are losing vital energy, unconsciously, most of the time. But this loss we must prevent; and we can. We can learn to hold, in our own system, all the energy we generate; and this may be accomplished in a very short time through the following exercise:

Take a few moments several times every day, and turn attention upon the energy that fills your physical and mental system. Then try to *feel* that you are holding all of this energy in your own system through the power of your mind. In fact, try to take conscious hold of this energy and keep it all in yourself. In a moment, you will feel more and more energy accumulating in every part of your being until you actually feel as if you were recharged. And you are. You have, for the time being, prevented all loss; and you are beginning to realize what a power you would become if you could always retain all the energy you generate. Repeat the exercise several times every day until it becomes second nature for your mind to hold within your own system all the energy you generate. Thus you prevent all loss permanently, and you will feel far stronger, both in mind and body, than ever before.

Full Supply.—Realizing the fact that the subconscious mind is the real source of energy, and that the subconscious will invariably respond to our conscious directions, we should make it a point to direct the subconscious every day to keep the system, physical and mental, absolutely full of vital energy every moment. This may be accomplished by turning attention upon the subconscious at frequent intervals, and actually declaring to the subconscious that this full supply be maintained. Results will positively follow.

Increase of Energy.—The permanent increase of vital energy may be secured by directing the subconscious to express, in mind and body, a larger supply. *The subconscious can*. The amount of latent energy in the great within is limitless; and, therefore, we may secure more and more as we desire. Turn the positive will upon the subconscious, and will to arouse more and more vital energy from within. *P*roceed calmly, and with determination; and fully expect to receive the increase that you have in mind.

The Aim in View.—We know the great law, that no ailment whatever can enter the human system, so long as that system is brim full of vital energy. Our aim in view therefore must be to possess, at a times, this full and abundant supply. And as we learn this great art, we shall always be well; we shall always be strong; we shall live a long, active life, and enjoy every moment to the highest degree.

CHAPTER II.
THE SUPER-PHYSICAL BREATH

Important Fact.—The physical atmosphere with which we are surrounded, and portions of which we inhale with every breath, is not composed of physical elements alone. And when we breathe, we take into the system something more besides the air that enters the lungs. The fact is, that the physical atmosphere is charged with certain vital forces, or life energies, that are drawn more or less into the physical system when we breathe; and that invariably tend to increase the vital energy of the system. In some localities the atmosphere contains more of this vital force than elsewhere; and we always find that the population of such localities feel stronger, more energetic and more alive, and accomplish a great deal more, both in the physical and the mental fields of activity. We also find that certain individuals have the happy faculty of drawing into their systems a greater supply than usual of this atmospheric life force, regardless of where they may live; and, in consequence; have far more energy, under every circumstance, than the majority.

The Energizing Breath.—It is not always convenient to select those localities where the atmosphere has the most energy; besides, the atmosphere in every locality may change its energy producing power with every change in climatic conditions. We cannot depend, therefore, upon conditions as they come and go in the external; but we can depend upon our own power to extract from the atmosphere all the life energy we may desire; for the fact is, that there is an abundance of this life energy in the atmosphere of any locality, regardless of climatic conditions; and we can, through the energizing breath, or the super-physical breath, draw into our systems as much of this force as we can hold or apply. This must become our purpose, therefore, because the human system does require a certain amount of this atmospheric energy in order to maintain perfect health. And when we can draw into the system a great deal more of this energy than is required for perfect health, we may increase remarkably both our working capacity and our joy of living. This latter fact is most evident, because it is when we feel as if we were literally charged with these highly refined life energies that life becomes nothing less than supreme joy. And it is then that we want to live for an indefinite period, and achieve wonderfully upon this planet.

The New Way.—In the usual way of breathing, we inhale what we can appropriate of the physical atmosphere, so as to supply certain demands of nature; and if the atmosphere happens to be well charged at the time, we draw into the system considerable life energy with every inhalation; but if the atmosphere does not happen to be well charged, we receive but a scant supply of this energy, and in consequence do not feel as strong or as well as usual. In the new way of breathing, however, we do not rely merely upon what energy may be received in the usual manner; we make a special effort to draw into the system an extra supply of life energy with every inhalation. And this we can readily do if we observe a few important laws in connection with general breathing and special exercises in breathing.

How to Begin.—Realize that the atmosphere you breathe is charged with certain vital energies and that a certain supply of these energies is taken into the system with every breath. Then realize that you can draw into your system a far greater supply of these energies; and that your body will have greater vitality and better health with every increase of this supply that you receive. The fact is, that, although your body may be too weak to move around, you can, by drawing more energy from the atmosphere into your system, make your body so strong and so vigorous that you will actually feel as if you were electrically charged through and through. You can, through the super-physical breath, restore your physical system to full health and vigor, no matter how low your vitality may be. And you can, in the same manner, increase your physical and mental power remarkably every year for an indefinite period.

General Exercise.—Whenever you breathe consciously, *think deeply* of the vital energy of the atmosphere; and as you inhale, desire with depth of feeling to draw more and more of this energy into your system with every breath. In ordinary physical breathing, the object is simply to secure oxygen for the lungs; but in *super physical breathing,* the object is to secure a greater and a greater supply of that finer life energy that permeates the atmosphere everywhere. And as you make a special and a conscious effort, in your general breathing, to attract more of this finer energy, you will soon develop the faculty of attracting more of this energy at all times, with every breath, whether you think of your breathing or not. The result will be that you will always have more energy than usual, and in every kind of atmosphere or climatic condition.

Special Exercise.—Be seated in a comfortable position, a position that will permit of a free and easy exercise of the lungs. See that there is an abundance of fresh air in the room. Then begin to breathe, gently and deeply, inhaling and exhaling slowly, holding the breath a few seconds after each inhalation, and being particular to note that the lungs are filled comfortably, through and through, with each succeeding inhalation. Continue this mode of breathing for ten or fifteen minutes, and as you do so turn your attention upon the finer life currents of the atmosphere. Try to get into *conscious touch* with the finer forces of these currents, and try to draw a goodly supply of those forces into your system with every inhalation. In this connection, it is most important to realize that the finer forces of the atmosphere that surround you will obey the desires of your mind. Therefore, if you place your mind and thought *in touch* with those forces, and *deeply desire* to draw them into your system as you inhale, those forces will actually obey; and you will receive a far greater supply of life energy from the atmosphere than usual.

The Chief Secret.—In order to draw more and more of this life force into your system as you breathe, the chief secret is to get your mind into such close contact with the finer side of that force, that you can actually feel it coming into every atom of your body with every breath. And this closer contact may be secured, by thinking deeply and frequently of the finer energies of the atmosphere, concentrating attention, as much as possible, upon that finer feeling in yourself that can feel the finer forces within you and about you. With practice and perseverance this finer feeling will come; and by using the mind in the attitude of that finer feeling, you can get into perfect touch with that finer force, thereby mastering the chief secret in the super-physical breath.

Further Information.—During this special exercise, try to draw an extra supply of atmospheric energy into your system with every inhalation; then as you hold your breath for a few seconds, try to feel that this finer energy is penetrating every fiber in your being, giving new life and vitality to every nerve and cell; and as you exhale, try to feel that all the extra energy received is *retained* in the system, as a permanent addition to your physical and mental power. Then inhale again, as before, repeating the entire process again and again, gently and in poise, for ten or fifteen minutes. At the close of this exercise, you will feel that you have a great deal more vitality in your system than you ever felt before, even though you did not get fully into the real secret of the exercise. But when you do get fully *into the real secret* of this exercise, you will actually feel like a "live wire," and you will feel strong enough "to move the world." However, do not permit yourself to be carried away. Be calm and continue in poise.

Positive Results.—This special exercise may be taken twice a day, preferably in the morning and early in the afternoon; but it is an excellent practice to employ the same process for a minute or two any time during the day when you have the opportunity. The result will be a steady increase of energy and vitality; and where the body is ailing, this increase of energy will soon provide you with sufficient health-giving vitality to eliminate completely every trace of disease, and restore your system absolutely to full health and vigor. And here it is well to repeat the great fact, that whenever the physical system becomes thoroughly filled with vital energy, it is impossible for any form of disease to remain in that system any more. When the room is filled with light, all darkness must entirely disappear. One of the great secrets to perfect health, therefore, is to fill the system thoroughly with vital energy; and super-physical breathing can positively do this under every circumstance.

Further Application.—The reason why we speak of this process as super-physical breathing is found in the fact that it deals with the attraction and appropriation of forces that are finer than the usual physical forces; and that it is a higher form of breathing added to the ordinary physical breathing. It is in every sense super-physical in its application; but it provides those finer life energies that alone can give the physical system that greater measure of vitality and force required for the highest state of vigorous health and power. It is therefore physical breathing extended, advanced and perfected to a much greater degree of effectiveness, and lifted up, so to speak, to a plane of action where we may draw upon the tremendous forces of nature in its finer and inexhaustible domains. This being true, we realize that the further application of the super-physical breath holds, within itself, most remarkable possibilities. We find that we may, through the simpler application of this breathing, supply the physical system with more and more vital energy until the body becomes strong enough to put every form of disease out of the way. And this is indeed a great achievement in itself. But when we find that we are surrounded with a limitless sea of inexhaustible energy, that permeates the atmosphere everywhere, and that we can learn to draw, more and more, upon this vast sea of energy through what we speak of as the super-physical breath, we realize what the further application of this great secret will mean. And our conclusion must be, that we will not delay this practice or study another day, but proceed at once to master this remarkable secret in every form and manner.

CHAPTER III.
PSYCHOLOGICAL EQUILIBRIUM

A Remarkable Fact.—If every man, woman and child in the world would attain to what we shall here speak of as psychological equilibrium, and would continue to live in that equilibrium, we should find, in less than a year, that more than ninety per cent of all the ailments of mankind would have disappeared completely.

The Reason Why.—The majority of all the ills that come to the human family have their origin, either in loss of vital energy, or in nervous conditions; that is, interior discord. But psychological equilibrium means *interior harmony* and balance; and therefore, when such an equilibrium is maintained, a nervous conditions and every form of nervousness will cease to exist in the system.

Wonderful Remedy.—Learn to live continually in a state of psychological equilibrium, and you will cure yourself absolutely of any and every nervous ailment you may have; and this is of vast importance, as there are very few people to be found that are not addicted to nervousness of some kind. And more than this: continue to live in this equilibrium, and you will avoid all nervous or mental ailments in the future. Your nerves will always be strong, and your mind in perfect harmony and balance. And here we should remember, that when the mind is always well the body will always be well.

A Personal Experiment.—Watch yourself closely for one whole day, with a view of ascertaining whether or not every element in your being has continued to act in perfect harmony and balance. In brief, ask yourself if you can actually feel harmonious in the within during that entire day. Then note the answer. If you do not feel harmonious in the within all through the day, you are addicted to nervousness; you are troubled with interior discord; and interior discord may, at any time, work itself out into all kinds of functional or organic ailments. But if you do feel harmonious in the within all through the day, you are living in a state of psychological equilibrium; and the spirit of health is abroad in every part of your system.

Remember This.—If you wish to be well, every organ in your body must perform its function perfectly; but no physical organ can perform its function perfectly unless it can act continually in a state of interior harmony and poise. The very moment you feel nervous, restless, agitated, disturbed or discordant in the within, you are undermining the natural and harmonious actions of your physical organs; and they will fail to do their duty. The result is that adverse conditions will arise, which, if not checked, may develop into serious ailments. It is absolutely necessary therefore to maintain interior harmony at all times, and such harmony may be realized through the attainment of psychological equilibrium.

The Two Sides.—There are two sides to the human system: the physiological and the psychological. And the latter governs the former. The physiological side is that part of the human system that can be weighed and measured. The psychological side is the interior, the intangible, the invisible; and, in brief, the sum total of all the forces, under-currents, feelings, emotions, chemical processes and interior activities that live and act and work in the body, but that are finer than the body, being composed, not of physical substance or matter, but of energies proceeding from mind and soul. And whenever the psychological side is disturbed, there will be a corresponding disturbance in the physiological; that is, any disturbance that you may feel in the within will produce a similar disturbance in the organs of the body, thereby preventing those organs from doing their work as they should.

The Ideal in View.—In the attainment of perfect health, our ideal in view must ever be to maintain that deep *interior harmony* and calm, wherein we feel that we are inwardly strong and inwardly serene at the same time—and at all times. Our aim must be to keep all the psychological factors within us in harmony and in balance, because this is indispensable to the highest degree of perfect health. The within must be charged with power, and alive through and through with perfect peace.

First Experiment.—Try for one whole day to feel exceedingly strong, and perfectly serene in the within. However active you may be with mind or body, try to feel this interior peace and power combine in your System every moment. But do not try hard. Simply know what you want to do; then know that you can. The experiment will be extremely interesting, and will mark a most important turning point in your life.

An Even Temper.—We all realize the value of an even temper if we wish to gain or retain perfect health; but an even temper is a state of mind that exists merely on the surface; it is a mere effect of deeper states of poise within. When we speak of the state of psychological equilibrium, however, we are dealing with the deepest state of feeling and life that we possess. We are dealing with those factors and forces within us that govern all physical conditions absolutely. And, therefore, we must have equilibrium, balance and harmony among the psychological factors before we can have equilibrium, balance and harmony among the physical factors. The body can be in order only when those finer and deeper forces within us, that govern the body, are in order. Physical health invariably proceeds from interior harmony; and when all the psychological or interior factors are in harmony, every cell in the body will be in perfect health.

General Exercise.—Form in your mind a clear idea of what the psychological factors really are. Then proceed to picture in your mind a state of being wherein all those factors are in harmony and equilibrium. Dwell deeply and constantly upon this mental picture until you can actually feel the spirit of this harmony and equilibrium gaining a deeper and deeper foothold in your system. In brief, try to live in the very soul of this interior state of perfect equilibrium; and try to realize the active presence of this state in every atom of your being. You will soon begin to feel the harmony you have in mind; and this feeling will become deeper and stronger every day until it becomes a permanent part of your consciousness.

Special Exercise.—Take ten minutes two or three times every day for the purpose of establishing permanently absolutely equilibrium, among the psychological factors, through the power of concentration; and proceed as follows:

Turn attention upon all the psychological factors in your system, including your feelings, your emotions, the under-currents of all the physical processes, the creative forces of mind and body, the interior workings of your system, the finer forces and elements in your personality, the mental life of every fibre and cell, the mentalities of all the organs in your body, and, briefly, everything in your system that you can think of as being psychological. Then group all of these factors in your imagination, by thinking of them as acting in a finer interior field within your system.

In other words, turn your attention upon the psychological field within your own personality. Then concentrate upon that field, with a deep, strong desire to feel and realize absolute harmony and equilibrium among all the elements and factors in that field. When concentrating, be calm, positive and determined; and hold in your mind the idea of *interior harmony* so deeply that the feeling of this harmony will penetrate every fibre, nerve and cell in your entire body. Thus you will steadily, and surely, create interior harmony throughout your entire system. You will establish psychological equilibrium among all the factors and elements within you; and when this equilibrium has become a permanent state in your deeper life, you will find that order, harmony and perfect health will be realized in your physical life.

Very Important.—Remember this, that so long as there is perfect harmony within you there will be perfect health in every nerve, fibre and cell in your system. The attainment of psychological equilibrium, therefore, is an attainment of the highest importance. But this interior harmony must be perfect.

CHAPTER IV.
NOURISHING THE BODY

First Rule.—When you enter the dining room, array yourself in the garment of joy. Forget your troubles, if you have any, and be happy. Talk happiness; think happiness; feel happiness; radiate happiness. Live in the spirit of mental sunshine, and give no serious thought to anything whatever. Light-heartedness and good cheer should prevail at this hour; and during this hour count it your privilege to eat, drink and be merry. And you can. Realize that when you are in the dining room you are in another world, away from problems, difficulties or weighty themes. You have come to enjoy a feast; so, therefore make it a feast in every sense of the term.

Second Rule.—Do not merely eat to live; and do not merely live to eat; there is a happy medium. Make your eating not the whole of your life, but a very important part of your life. Enjoy your meals; and enjoy them thoroughly. A meal that is thoroughly enjoyed will be thoroughly digested. *P*lease remember this great fact. And it is a great fact, for a perfect digestion is not only necessary to the best expression of the body, but also to the best expression of the mind and the soul. Everything in your system works better when digestion is good. And as the body is the instrument of mind and soul, it is clearly evident that mind and soul can act as they should only when the body is in perfect condition. The piano must be perfectly tuned if the music is to be perfect in harmony and superior in quality. Think of your body as a musical instrument. Then remember that the perfect harmony of that instrument *depends so much* on a perfect digestion; and realize that every meal will be thoroughly digested if thoroughly enjoyed.

Third Rule.—In making the proper selection of your food, do not be too particular. See that the food is nourishing, wholesome, clean and correctly prepared. Then make up your mind to enjoy it all to the full. Do not go to the table in a fault-finding attitude. So long as you are in that attitude you cannot digest anything. Your indigestion, therefore, will not be the result of your food, but the result of your disagreeable state of mind. Remember, that a disagreeable state of mind can upset your entire system, and even convert the digestive juices of your system into poisonous elements. So do not blame the food. Most food is harmless. But see that your mind is right before you enter the dining room. Never eat when cross, upset, agitated, nervous, worried or in a state of fear. Throw these things off. First, *get your mind right*. Turn on a goodly supply of mental sunshine, and be glad. And by all means, never get into the habit of thinking that you cannot eat "this" or digest "that." The fact is you can eat anything that is wholesome and nourishing; and you can digest every bit of it, if you think so, and partake of your meals in the spirit of sunshine and joy.

Fourth Rule.—When you are in the dining room, take your time. Hurried eating means nothing but loss all along the line. Hurried meals are never digested perfectly; so, therefore, they nourish the system but in part, and they lead to many ailments, which means loss of time, money and pleasure. When your meals are properly digested, you can accomplish more in one hour than you can in three when digestion is not good. Sufficient time for your meals, therefore, is a good investment, both for the present and the future. Take a the time necessary to fully enjoy your meals, and permit mind and body to remain relaxed and care-free for about thirty minutes more. You owe this time to your body. *Be good to your physical body*. It is your duty and your privilege. If your body is treated well it will serve you long and serve you well; and, in addition, contribute immensely to the joys of existence.

Fifth Rule.—Consider the entire process of digestion, and remember that this process begins the very moment you can taste your food. Therefore, do not ignore this first part of the process. On the contrary, continue to taste your food as long as you can; that is, continue to masticate every mouthful as long as it can be tasted. This is one of the most important secrets to a perfect digestion. It matters not how weak your stomach may be, if you continue to masticate every mouthful as long as it can be tasted, and eat moderately, the entire meal will be we digested. And your stomach will gain in strength every day, until perfect health and vigor is regained. In addition to this, it is a fact that a thoroughly masticated meal will give from ten to one hundred per cent more nourishment to the body than a meal partaken of in the usual manner. And the better you nourish your body the better will be your health, the stronger you will be, both physically and mentally, the longer you will live, and the easier you will find it to stay young as long as you live.

Sixth Rule.—It is highly important that the circulation be fully and vigorous throughout the digestive system. A full circulation will not only promote digestion, but will also give a more immediate and a more perfect distribution to the nourishing elements secured from the food. This matter, therefore, should receive our best attention, and we shall find it an excellent practice to concentrate the mind, gently and peacefully, upon the abdominal region, for a few moments preceding every meal. During this concentration we should deeply desire the increase of the circulation throughout that region, and we should try to *feel* that increase actually taking place. This simple method will add remarkably to the vigor of the digestive organs; and this method alone will cure almost any ailment of the digestive system. It will always give relief; and when combined with the other secrets to good health, will cure every ailment that may be connected with the digestive process in any form or manner. If there seems to be considerable difficulty with digestion this method may also be applied for a few moments immediately after each meal. And when the digestive organs do not act as nature intended, use this method thoroughly, several times every day. Concentrate deeply, with a will, especially upon the lower parts of the abdominal region, and *deeply feel* the desired action taking place. Make it a point at all times to see that your circulation is full and vigorous all through your body. There is nothing that will do more than a good circulation to keep the body clean, wholesome and well. And you can increase the circulation in any part of your body through right and harmonious use of mind, thought, feeling, concentration and will.

Seventh Rule.—To nourish the body properly it is not necessary to adopt any particular system of diet. Anything that is wholesome and properly prepared may be partaken of freely, if partaken of in joy. Never be a "crank" about your food. A "cranky mind" is an enemy to good digestion; and you will find that people who are following "fads" in foods, are forever "dieting" to keep their digestion in order. Take the common sense way and select freely from a kinds of food, always selecting the wholesome and the clean. Then eat, *in the spirit of good cheer,* what your system seems to require, and think of it all as good—very good. Eat what you want, but only as much as you need, and enjoy every meal as you would a royal feast. In fact, think of every meal as a royal feast, and so it will be to you.

Eighth Rule.—Think of your food as not merely having physical elements, but also finer elements. A food is charged, so to speak, with finer elements and energies; and, if we recognize these in our own minds, at every meal, we will assimilate them more thoroughly, and thereby add remarkably to the vitality of the system. Train your mind to think of your food as having, stored up in every atom, life-giving energies, in addition to nourishing properties and elements; and you will soon find that every meal will give you far more energy, vitality and working capacity than you ever realized before. In addition, you will find yourself gaining more and more of that *finer force* that makes the human personality something more than a physical body with a nervous system. And, as we all desire our personalities to attain that "something more" state of being, this part of our theme will be found extremely important.

CHAPTER V.
NOURISHING THE MIND

Fundamental Law.—As the mind is, so is also the body. When the mind is in order, the body will be in order, and *vice versa*. When the mind is in good health, the body will be in good health. When the mind begins to lose hold upon life, the body will gradually weaken until personal existence cannot be maintained any longer. When the mind lays hold upon more and more life, the body will steadily gain in the possession of life, until there is sufficient life and vitality, in every organ in the body, to eliminate every ailment in the present, and prevent all ailments in the future. When the mind is young, the body will be young. And whatever is realized in the mind will be expressed through the body. See that the mind is right, and all else will be right in the human system.

Leading Essential.—To keep the mind right, every part of the mind must be properly nourished. And the real secret in nourishing the mind is to see that every part of the mind is constantly interested in the new, the larger and the higher. In the body, it is nourishment that produces growth; in the mind, *it is growth that produces nourishment.*

Food for the Mind.—It is new thought that constitutes the proper food for the mind; and the more new thought the mind is given the privilege to create, the better the mind will be nourished. To create new thought the mind must constantly advance towards the new, into the new, and up into the larger and the higher. And such an advancement can only follow a deep, strong and ceaseless interest in the new, the superior, and the most perfect everywhere.

Mental Expansion.—If mental expansion be made perpetual, health will become perpetual, and youth will become perpetual. The body cannot become old so long as the mind continues to grow; and as long as every part of the mind is active and alive, every part of the body will be strong, wholesome and well. When parts of the mind become inactive, groups of cells here and there in many parts of the body will also become inactive; and inactive cells not only become obstacles to the natural functions of the body, but these cells will soon harden and ossify. And it is the hardening of the cells that produces old age. The hardening of the cells also produces many ailments, because nature cannot do its work properly when dead and hardened cells are scattered in groups here and there all through the body. It is impossible, however, for a single cell in the body to harden or ossify so long as every part of the mind is alive. The mind is in vital touch with every cell, fibre and atom in the physical body; and as every cell responds absolutely to the actions of the mind, no cell can be dead so long as every part of the mind is alive.

The Growing Mind.—To keep every part of the mind alive, the whole mind must be well nourished; and the only mind that is well nourished is the growing mind. *The mind feeds on change.* The mind that does not change will starve; and when the mind starves the body dries up, withers, becomes old and ossified. This condition may take place however well the body may be nourished; for, although it is well to give proper nourishment to the body, it is more important to give proper nourishment to the mind.

Very Important.—We must remember this, and remember it well, that every cell in the body is closely connected, through the nervous system, with the mind; and also that every cell is directly influenced by the mind. In fact, all the cells in the body tend to act as the mind acts, tend to become what the mind becomes, and tend to change or improve as the mind improves. Therefore, if certain parts of the mind should become inactive, a great many of the cells in the body would also fall into inactivity. And an inactive cell soon becomes a dead, hardened or ossified cell, which means the coming of disease, old age or inability in one or many ways. It is absolutely necessary, therefore, if we wish to retain health and youth, that every part of the mind be alive—that the whole mind continue to grow, expand and develop perpetually.

Practical Methods.—In the first place, remember the great law, *renew your mind and be well.* And to renew the mind we must be interested in the new—deeply and vitally interested in the new along all lines. We must learn to live for the growing, advancing, expanding life; and we must become enthused over every step in progress that the race may take, in any direction, or under any circumstance. Everything that is new must arouse and attract our attention; and we must keep our eyes open to the new, everywhere, with an interest that is thoroughly alive, and thoroughly wide awake in every form and manner. In brief, we must develop *an intense passion for the new*—the new in a things, and the new in higher and greater things. The entire soul must be aroused with a ceaseless desire to realize the new, and to change perpetually into more perfect states and degrees of the new. And this process must become a positive force in the system—so positive and so strong that every fiber and cell is thrilled with the spirit of a new life.

First Exercise.—The first thing to do is to wake up the mind—every part of the mind. And remember that the moment every part of the mind is thoroughly wide awake, every cell in the body will be thoroughly alive. This means the coming of good health, for when all the cells in the body are thoroughly alive, there can be no disease in that body whatever. A cell that is alive cannot be sick. It is the dead cells and hardened cells that cause all the trouble. But when all the cells are alive, there will be no dead or hardened cells to give the body trouble; and, in consequence, health, order and harmony will prevail throughout the system. To proceed, apply the will upon every part of the mind, with a deep, strong desire to become mentally wide awake in every form and manner. Continue this process for a few moments, and repeat several times every day. The result of this simple exercise alone will, in a very short time, renew the entire body; for the fact is, that an awakened mind will renew itself very quickly; and when the mind is renewed, the body is renewed in a similar manner.

Special Exercise.—Make it your purpose to look for the new everywhere, in all things, and at all times. And awaken within yourself a deeper and a stronger interest in every manifestation of the new. Try to interest every part of your mind in the new along all lines; and try to arouse your whole mind to become wide awake to the force of growth and progress at work in all the world. Whenever you have a moment to spare, think of the new; think of new possibilities and new developments; and engage your attention, with the greatest enthusiasm, in everything new you can observe at the time. The effect will be remarkable, as it will not only awaken many parts of the mind that have heretofore been dormant, but will also train the mind in the art of discerning the new, the larger and the greater in all things. And it is such a mind that will become a growing mind, which is most important because *so long as the mind continues to grow, the body will continue to be well.*

An Excellent Practice.—Begin the day by resolving to see how many new things you can find during the day. Also begin the day by resolving to think more new things than you ever thought of in any day in the past. This will keep the mind awake to the new a through the day; and the mind that is continually wide awake to the new will continue to be a growing mind. This same practice will make every part of the mind more and more alive; and this means that every cell in the body will become more and more alive—the very purpose we have in view; for it is absolutely impossible for a cell to be sick that is thoroughly alive. And here it is well to repeat that it is impossible for the body to get sick or get old so long as the mind continues to grow. The growing mind is the one great preventative for sickness or age; and the growing mind is the greatest remedy of all, whatever the ailment or difficulty may be. See that your mind continues every day, and every hour, to be a growing mind, and you will always have health and youth, no matter how long you may live.

The Great Law.—Everything must be nourished if it is to continue to live; *and everything will continue to live so long as it is properly nourished.* But the mind of man has not been properly nourished; accordingly, the mind has weakened from year to year; and what happens to the mind happens to the body also. *F*rom this weakness, or lack of abundant life, has come ailments and age, all of which could have been prevented through the proper nourishment of the mind. The mind, however, is not nourished by what comes from without, or by what may be received from external sources. It is new thought alone that can nourish the mind; and the only thought that is new to any individual mind is the thought created by that mind itself while in search of the new. The great secret, therefore, in nourishing the mind is to train the whole mind to develop *an intense passion for the new.*—the new in all things, from the most simple to the most sublime. Such a mind will indeed be a growing mind; and so long as the mind continues to grow the body will continue to be well. And, also, if mental expansion be made perpetual, health will become perpetual, and youth will become perpetual.

CHAPTER VI.
THE WILL TO BE WELL

Know the Will.—We must understand the will, and its true function, if we would always be well. And the reason is evident. The will is one of the most important factors in the human system, and contains, within itself, powers and possibilities that the majority have never called forth into action at any time. These powers, however, can, when applied, turn the tide of life in our favor, no matter what the difficulties or circumstances may be. And this is especially true in the realization of perfect health.

The Power of Will.—We must always will to act before we can act, whether the action be physical or mental. And the more we express in the action the more powerful and effective will that action be. Whatever we do, therefore, results will depend largely upon how much will we give to the work or purpose in hand. This being true, we should always turn on the full current of the will. We should never act in a half-hearted way, but should invariably act with all the power and will we possess. We should always will to be our best, and will to do our best. The increase, when we come to measure results will be very great indeed.

Important Fact.—The more will you apply along any line of action, the more energy and power you cause to flow into the same line of action. Continue to will, with force, determination and persistence, upon any purpose or project, and you will gradually draw more and more energy into that purpose, until all the power within you is working with you, and for you, in the realization of that purpose. Then you can certainly get results, the greatest and best results possible.

Will to Be Well.—The same rule holds good in your purpose to gain health, or build up a greater measure of health. *Will to be well;* and you cause all the energies within you to work for better and better health. *Will to be strong;* and you aid nature, both directly and indirectly, in building up the strength, the vigor and the virility of your entire system. Turn on the full current of the will, and you aid nature immensely. You turn the tide of life in your own favor. You inspire all the elements and forces within you to leave the side of weakness, and go over to the side of life, power and strength. You turn conditions round about completely, so that the things that were against you will henceforth be for you. You can do all these things, if you use the will—the full current of the will, and always will to be what you want to be.

First Exercise.—Take positive hold of your will, and be determined, henceforth, to apply the full power of the will—and always for more life, for more energy, for greater strength, for better health, and for everything that can add to your greatest welfare and highest good. Take hold of the will in this way, many times every day; and in every instance feel deeply, and be tremendously in earnest.

Second Exercise.—Turn the power of the will upon all the conditions of your health; and train yourself, more and more, to will greater vitality and better health into every part of your system. And whenever you use the will feel deeply. Try to feel that the force of your will comes forth from the great and invincible powers of the soul; and try to feel that whatever you will to realize or attain must come to pass. The power of the soul can never fail; and your will—*your true will*—is the power of the soul in positive, determined expression.

Third Exercise.—Turn the power of the will upon that part of your body that may need better health. Then *will* more and more life, power and health into, and *through,* that part of the body, until you can actually feel every cell thrill with vigor and virility. Think of that part of the body, with depth of feeling, and *will to be well*. Concentrate all your thought, and the full power of mind and soul, upon that part of the body, and *will to be well*. And know that the power of your will comes from the limitless power of your own invincible soul. You may therefore have unbounded faith in what you are doing, because you *know* that the results you desire must positively follow.

The Strong Mind.—Whenever you think, or use your mind in any form or manner, use more and more of the will. Make your entire mental world positive and strong. And always remember to combine *deep feeling* with every exercise or expression of the will. This is most important, because the deeper the feeling, the stronger the will under every circumstance. And a strong, deep will means a strong mind; which, in turn, means greater power of mind over all physical conditions. The mind is by right the master over the body. Therefore, the stronger the mind becomes the greater becomes your power to master and regulate every part of your body. And this is a power we all want to possess. When the mind can control the body perfectly, then we may always have perfect health, an unlimited amount of vitality, and an abundance of rich, wholesome, energizing life.

Personal Power.—Use the full power of the will upon your entire personality. Make your personality strong, positive, alive. Will to have more personal power. Will to express more personal power in every movement of the body, in every feeling of the mind, and in every action of the soul. Will more life and more energy into every cell in your body, into every nerve, into every fiber, into every force, into every function. *Be determined to be personally strong and virile.* And use the full power of the will with this important end in view. The result will be that you will gain in every form and manner, especially in vigor and in health. When you apply the full power of the will upon every part of the personality, you arouse, to positive action, all the vital energies within you; and when your personality is thoroughly alive, it is absolutely impossible for any ailment whatever to enter your system.

Do Not Give In.—When conditions in your system seem adverse, do not permit yourself to ever think of giving up, or giving in. Will to *pull through*. For the fact is, that so long as you hold on, with the full power of will, the forces of life in your system will be *on your side* working in your favor. The forces in your system *will never give up* so long as you refuse to give up. And there is no condition in your system that the forces of life, in your system, cannot overcome if you give them sufficient time, continuous encouragement, and the full force of your own determined will. Will to stand by the powers within you, under every circumstance, and those powers will stand by you. They will positively see you through; and you will come out with full victory, and with a greater realization of freedom than you ever knew before.

Most Important.—Train your mind to realize, more and more deeply, that will power is soul power; that the real power of the will comes from the soul; and that the soul is positively invincible. Then proceed, in this realization *to will to be well*. Continue, under every circumstance, to will to be well, knowing that the limitless power of the soul is back of your will, in your will, and working positively, with full force, through your will.

Special Exercise.—Take several moments, three or four times every day, and give special attention to the making of the will stronger, deeper and more positive. First, simply *will* to will more; that is, think of your will, knowing what it is, and determine to express more of the power of will in every act of the will. This, in itself, will, even in a few days, strengthen the will remarkably; and you will find that you can give a great deal more power and effective action to everything you purpose or undertake. Second, concentrate the will, with deep feeling and more determined action, upon the various faculties and qualities in your mind, and upon the various functions in your personality. In fact, proceed to train the mind to express more will *into everything* in your entire system. Third, direct your subconscious mind to give greater force, greater volume, greater positiveness, greater power, and deeper action to every expression of your will. This is most important; and here we should remember, that the *subconscious will invariably does* whatever it is directed to do, provided we feel deeply when we give the directions, and continue to be tremendously in earnest.

Gaining Ground.—The more you apply the foregoing methods and principles, the stronger and deeper will the will become. And as the will develops in force, positiveness and power, you will find that you will gain ground continually in the building up of mind and body, provided you make it the great rule of your life—*to will to be well.* And results will increase the more deeply you feel that the limitless power of the soul is back of your will, in your will, and working positively, with full force, through your will.

CHAPTER VII.
INTERIOR RELAXATION

The First Principle.—Nature demands recuperation. If all the functions of nature are to perform their duties properly, there must be periods set aside, every day, for complete recuperation. The energies that have been utilized must be replaced; and the cells that have served their purpose must be eliminated, and new ones built up instead. In brief, the entire physical and mental system must be reconstructed and made over new; and all the natural processes of repair, renewal and reconstruction must be given the opportunity to complete their work thoroughly, at least once in every twenty-four hours. And this opportunity, when fully realized, constitutes complete recuperation.

Important Fact.—If the entire human system were given the opportunity to recuperate thoroughly at least once every day, it would be impossible for disease of any kind to enter the system; and conditions of old age could never gain a foothold in a single organ or cell in the body. And the reason why is this, that complete recuperation would mean, first, complete renewal of all the cells; and second, the thorough recharging of every part of the system with vital energy. Thus the two great essentials to health and youth would be provided, because it is impossible for any kind of disease to enter the human system so long as there is a full supply of vital energy; and it is impossible for old age conditions to gain a foothold anywhere so long as nature is given the privilege to renew *every cell* in the system the very moment the former cell has fully served its purpose.

The Second Principle.—Complete recuperation of mind and body can take place only when the entire human system is thoroughly relaxed; and relaxation is thorough only when it becomes, what we may well term, *interior relaxation.* That is, the process of relaxation must originate in the within, or on the subconscious side of life, and must penetrate, in every form and manner, both the interior and the exterior phases of the personality.

Meaning of Relaxation.—In the usual state of conscious activity, the human system continues to give expression to all its forces and elements. The exterior side of the personality is in a positive attitude, and all life and power moves from the within towards the without. In other words, all the energies of the system are going out into, and through, the various organs, to carry out the active functions of mind and body; and in this process a large part of the available energy is utilized, and many of the cells complete their period of usefulness. But when relaxation takes place, the course of action in the system is reversed; that is, all the elements and forces of the system move from the without towards the within. The process of expression discontinues, and the exterior phase of the personality becomes passive instead of positive.

General Exercise.—Whenever you wish to relax, turn attention towards the within, or towards the subconscious, and "let go," fully expecting all the forces of your system to turn about and move, gently and peacefully, toward a state of interior calm. In a few moments you will feel relaxed all the way through, and a serene, restful feeling will gradually come over your entire personality. This exercise can be taken to advantage, for five or ten minutes every two or three hours during the day; and should be taken, with unfailing punctuality before every meal, regardless of time, place or circumstance.

Results.—The value of this exercise will be found in the realization of renewed supply of life and energy, at frequent intervals, which means that power and capacity will continue to be up to the mark all through the day; and this will mean more work and better work invariably. And when this exercise is taken before meals, the system will be recharged with vitality, so that the process of digestion can be carried on perfectly. In fact, if you relax thoroughly, for five minutes, before every meal, you can say farewell, for all time, to all kinds of ailments or annoyances in your digestive functions.

The Third Principle.—The human system is repaired, renewed and recharged by the subconscious side of life. And in order that these necessary processes may take place, there are two essentials that must be provided. First, the exterior phases of every cell must be passive; and, second consciousness must function principally through the interior phases of every cell at the time. And these two essentials are provided perfectly when we are in a state of *interior relaxation*. That is, when we relax, the outer side of life becomes passive; positive expression is discontinued; the working forces are withdrawn from the external elements of the personality, and our conscious actions are "let go" so that all our feelings are permitted to "sink in" to the deeper subconscious life, where all is peaceful and serene. And here it is well to remember that the subconscious always works in perfect peace. Subconscious activity is absolutely still at all times, so therefore you may know that when you feel deeply, and feel absolutely still in the within, the subconscious side of your life is doing its work perfectly. And this is the state you should enter when you are to realize *interior relaxation*.

Relax Before Sleep.—We can enjoy sleep only when we relax thoroughly for some time before going to sleep. In many instances, nature is able to provide perfect relaxation just as we are falling asleep; but nature has been interfered with in so many ways, that many of the natural processes do not perform their functions properly unless assisted by mind or thought. We should provide this assistance, therefore, by making it a practice to enter a state of *interior relaxation* for at least ten minutes before we are ready to go to sleep. And we shall find that the purpose of sleep will, in this simple practice, be realized to the fullest and the most perfect degree.

Special Exercise.—Take thirty minutes every day, preferably early in the evening, or during the latter part of the afternoon, for the purpose of entering completely into a perfect state of *interior relaxation*. Begin by turning attention upon the within. Know that the within is always peaceful and still; and know that your own mind and personality will also become peaceful and still the moment you come in conscious touch with the within. Then "let go." Try to feel that all the forces within you are moving towards the serenity and calm of the subconscious side. Breathe peacefully and gently at the time, and as you "let go" of the contents of your lungs with each exhalation, also "let go" of your own feelings—letting them "sink in" to the stillness of the within. Continue by *thinking* quietly of your external personality as being perfectly passive; and picture in your mind, as clearly as possible, the forces of your system, *moving inwardly,* gently, serenely, towards the subconscious side. Repeat these various processes, in the deep, quiet faith that perfect and *interior relaxation* is being realized. Gradually, you will find your conscious feeling in a state where you can actually *feel* that your interior life is fully relaxed; and this is the real purpose you have in view.

Further Exercise.—Your object should be to become so familiar with the state of *interior relaxation,* that you can actually see a mental picture of this state whenever you so desire. For the fact is, that whatever you can picture in your mind, that you can realize at any time. In other words, when you can "mentally see" a perfect state of *interior relaxation,* all you need to do is to turn your attention upon that mental picture whenever you wish to enter the relaxed state. The elements and forces within you always proceed at once to do whatever you can perfectly picture in your mind as doing. It is highly important, therefore, to learn to "mentally see" the relaxed state as you know it to be.

Special Information.—When you are not in good health, it is most important that you relax more frequently, not less than three or four times every day. And as you relax, concentrate subjectively upon that part of the body that may lack in health and vigor. When you concentrate subjectively upon any part of the body, you *think* of the finer life that permeates the physical side; and therefore, if you relax at the same time, you will cause the processes of repair, renewal and recuperation to work more perfectly and more quickly in that part of the body, thereby hastening recovery to a marked degree. In fact, when subjective concentration and interior relaxation are combined upon that part of the body that is ailing, it is possible to secure complete recovery in one-half, or even in one-fourth, the time usually required by nature herself under similar circumstances. We can truthfully say, therefore, that these two great factors—*subjective concentration and interior relaxation*—when perfectly combined, constitute one of the greatest curative agents known to modern science. And they who will learn to apply these two factors perfectly, in combination, will acquire a secret, the value of which will be nothing less than extraordinary.

CHAPTER VIII.
IMAGINE YOURSELF WELL

The Principle.—The mind always creates what we imagine; and it is the imaging faculty that determines what we are to think. We are as we think; and we think as we imagine. Therefore, if we are to think as we wish to think, and be what we wish to be, we must first learn to use the imaging faculty according to fundamental principle and exact science.

The First Rule.—Continue to imagine, under every circumstance, what you wish to become, gain or realize; but never imagine, for a moment, what you do not want. Train your imagination, in a most positive manner, every day, to comply with this rule; and gradually you will find that all the conditions of mind and body are becoming more and more as you wish them to be.

General Exercise.—Form a mental picture of yourself, in your imagination, as you wish to be in mind and body. See yourself well and strong with the eye of the mind. Imagine that you have become what you wish to be; and try to feel, through and through, what you have imagined. Train your mind to enter as deeply as possible into every correct move you make with the imagination, and be determined to see and feel the perfect picture you have formed of yourself. Make a special effort, to this end, many times every day, and in fact, whenever you have a moment to spare. Think of this perfect picture of yourself, as frequently as possible, as much as possible, and as deeply as possible. And be tremendously in earnest.

Important Fact.—The human system is constantly filled with creative energies; these energies are at work night and day, building and creating; and they always select those things, as their patterns, that we imagine with the deepest of feeling and the greatest of force. Imagine yourself sick, and if you give much force and feeling to that imagination, the creative energies within you will thereby create, in your system, the very ailment you imagine that you have. In like manner, imagine yourself perfectly well, and those same energies will proceed at once to create perfect health in every part of your system. But your imagination must be positive, deeply felt and thoroughly alive through and through. Imagine any condition in yourself, and the creative energies will create that condition, provided the imagination be deep, vivid and intense. This fact proves that the power of imagination is a marvelous power—in truth, the greatest there is in man.

Remember This.—More than ninety per cent of the ailments that appear in the human system come largely from the misuse of the imagination. And it is a positive fact that no sickness could appear in the life of any living entity where the power of imagination was applied in a positive, wholesome and constructive manner during every moment of existence.

The Great Law.—When the imagination of man is right, everything in the life of man will be right. When we imagine only the true, the perfect and the ideal, we shall constantly grow into higher and higher realizations of the true, the perfect and the ideal. Thus we gain freedom from the lesser or the wrong by constantly rising into the greater and the right.

Special Exercise.—Take ten or fifteen minutes of silence, preferably alone. Turn your attention upon the great within of your own mind and soul. Then picture, in the within, the perfect form of health and power that you wish to realize in your external personality. Think of this perfect picture, so deeply, and so vividly, that you can actually see it in the light of your own marvelous imagination. And having formed the picture in the within, proceed to concentrate upon that picture with all the mental power you possess. Focus attention so absolutely upon that picture, in the within, that you know nothing else whatever for the time being. Persevere until your concentration becomes perfect; and repeat the exercise two or three times every day. The result of this exercise will be that you will actually create, in the within, that very form, or new creation, upon which you concentrate with such determination and mental power. And whatever we create in the within will positively express itself in the outer personality.

Remarkable Law.—Concentrate mind, thought and feeling upon any condition in your system, and you create that condition invariably, provided the power of concentration is directed inwardly, and repeated frequently, with a the power you possess.

Interesting Experiment.—Turn your attention upon the great within, and picture, in the within, a counterpart of yourself having all the elements, qualities and appearance of external youth. In brief, imagine the *internal existence* of a new physical form—young, vigorous, virile—alive with the fire and splendor of youth. Then concentrate upon this internal form of virility and youth, in the same deep and powerful manner, as was indicated in the preceding exercise. Repeat many times every day; and the result will be that you will actually create, in the within, another personality—a personality with youth, life and power. And gradually this young personality, from within, will come forth into the outer physical form, and cause the outer physical form to regain, in every mode and manner, a the elements, conditions and powers of youth. In brief, the newly created personality of youth and virility from within will remove all the conditions of age that may exist in the outer personality, just as darkness is dispelled by the light; and will thereby restore natural youth to the physical body—something to which every physical form is entitled as long as life continues in that form. The possibility of this law is extraordinary—in fact, limitless in its own field; and the truth is, that any man, even though he might have the appearance of ninety, could regain the appearance of thirty five if he would apply, in a thorough and effective manner, the full power of this remarkable law.

The Unfailing Truth.—Whatever we create in the within, the same will positively express itself in the outer personality. And the creative energies within can create any condition or quality we desire, provided they are properly directed by the marvelous power of imagination.

Curative Power.—The fact is that the creative energies in your system can restore any part of your body to perfect health. The curative power of those energies is positively limitless. But they must be given the proper direction; and this imagination alone can do. *P*roceed by turning your attention to that part of the body that is ailing. Then imagine that part of the body *perfectly well*. Proceed farther, by trying to see and *feel* what you imagine; that is, imagine that you see every fiber perfect and whole; and imagine that you *feel* perfectly well throughout that part of your system. *P*roceed still farther by concentrating all the power of mind and soul upon what you now imagine in that part of your body. Focus attention absolutely upon what you now see and feel in that organ or muscle or nerve; and the very thing you imagine, that you will create. You will create perfect health and a super-abundance of vital energy at the very point where your concentration is directed. These are the results that you will positively secure; but your feeling must be deep; your concentration must be absolute; your imagination must be perfect; and you must be tremendously in earnest.

Vitally Important.—Never use the power of imagination, at any time, for any other purpose than that of building for the true, the perfect and the ideal in yourself, in your life, in your world. Imagine always the higher, the greater, the wonderful, the sublime. Train your imagination to look towards the heights and create the richness and the glory of the heights for every part of your world, here and now.

CHAPTER IX.
THE REAL LIVING OF LIFE

First Rule.—Learn to live more. All power comes from life. To increase power, physical or mental, we must increase life; and we increase life by constantly living more.

Second Rule.—Learn to give a more positive expression of life into every part of body, mind and soul. To live more we must express more life through every channel of consciousness; and this expression must be positive and strong, and at the same time perfectly poised and deeply serene.

Third Rule.—Learn to feel the real, interior action of life, at all times, and in every part of the system. To live more life we must feel more deeply the reality of life itself; that is, our conscious feeling must penetrate into the very spirit of life so that we can actually realize ourselves in the limitless life-current.

Important Fact.—We do not really live until we can feel the limitless life-current pulsating in every fiber and vein. We do not really live until we live in the very *spirit* of life; and to live in the spirit of life is to feel, through and through, the power of ceaseless, limitless, invincible life.

Remember This.—All ailments, of whatever nature, can be traced to insufficient life. But it is impossible for any ailment to enter the system, under any circumstances, so long as there is an abundance of life. And to maintain an abundance of life, the law is, to constantly live more.

Fourth Rule.—In order to live more, we must place ourselves in perfect harmony with the law of advancement. The soul was made to advance continuously—to move upward and onward eternally; and therefore we are not true to the soul unless we so live that this advancement of the soul may be promoted, in the fullest and most thorough manner, without any interruption whatever. And to promote this continuous advancement of the soul we must enter, more and more perfectly, into the spirit of life—into the *interior force* of the great invincible life current. This current is forever moving forward into more life, into a larger life, into a higher life, into a greater and more powerful life; and we may move upward and onward with this current if we learn to live, more and more deeply, in the very spirit of real life.

The Real Cause.—If we should undertake to trace any particular ailment back to its real cause, we would find that cause to be the advancement of life coming to a full stop. For the fact is, that whenever we come to a full stop in our advancement or growth, we lose hold upon the real life current; that is, we step aside from the life current, and, for the time being, are not filled with the life of that current. The result is that we fail to receive our full supply of life; the life force within us is not replenished at the time, and our supply is not sufficient to carry on, in a perfect manner, the natural functions of existence. Accordingly, conditions arise in the system that may lead to physical ailments, mental inefficiency, or adversity and wrong in general. To state it briefly, we cause our supply of life to diminish whenever we come to a stop in our growth or advancement, because whenever we make such a stop, we step aside from the life-current, and, therefore, are not receiving our supply of life at the time. And whenever we diminish our natural supply of life we make it impossible for mind and body to perform their functions perfectly. The consequences will be that ailments, wrongs and troubles of many kinds will follow.

The Great Law.—Continue to advance in the within—in the soul-during every moment of existence. Do not come to a stop at any time, or under any circumstance. The purpose of life is to move upward and onward eternally. Be true to that purpose, and you will ever receive more and more life. Continue to live and move and have your being in the very spirit of the *great life current*; do not step aside for a moment. Be in that current eternally, and you will always be filled, through and through, with all the life you can realize, appropriate and apply.

Fifth Rule.—If you do not realize at once the existence of the life-current within you, proceed to imagine the interior existence of that current. Make this imagination so clear and so vivid that you can actually *see* that current moving upward and onward eternally, and with invincible force, through the entire domain of your soul. Then imagine that *you are in* that current, moving with that current into more and more of the one invincible, limitless life. Proceed more deeply into this realization, and imagine that you actually *feel* the full force of that life and that current in every fiber and vein. The result will be, that you will enter more and more deeply into the very spirit of limitless life. You will then be *in* the full force of limitless life; and when you are in that life you will be so full of life that there will be no room, anywhere in your system, for discord, ailments, weakness or wrong. You will have turned on the full light of life and power, and all darkness will have disappeared completely.

Deep Feeling.—Know the truth that there is within you the force and power of limitless life—that a great, invincible life-current is eternally passing through your soul, giving more and more life to every element in your soul. Know this great truth; then proceed to *feel,* more and more deeply, the very spirit of this wonderful life-current. And the more deeply you feel this current, the more thoroughly you will enter into the full force and power of that current. You will constantly receive more and more every moment; and to *live more,* that is the secret to complete emancipation. Give more life to every atom in your system, and your entire system will become pure, wholesome, vigorous, powerful, virile and absolutely well.

The True Life.—When we enter into the spirit of the full life and the real life within us, then indeed shall we begin to live the true life—the life that is ever becoming larger, richer, more perfect, more beautiful, more ideal. We shall not only gain health and freedom, but shall, as well, gain more and more of all that is worthy and desirable in human existence. But we must first gain possession of more life. We must first learn to live more, and forever more. We must first learn to live and move and have our being in the great life-current—the limitless life that is a within us and all about us everywhere. And to learn these things we must place ourselves in perfect harmony with that great law of the soul that is ever prompting all life to move upward and onward forever. We must live constantly in the spirit of this law so that we may enter, every moment, into the deeper life, the larger life, the richer life, the greater life, the more spiritual life. Our living must become *real living;* and in real living there is peace, there is power, there is purity, there is wholeness, there is freedom; and there is perpetual increase of *real* life, and of all that is worthy and good in life. The great secret then is this, *enter forever and ever into more life.* Then all that is good must inevitably follow—and in a constantly increasing measure.

CHAPTER X.
THE RIGHT USE OF BODY, MIND AND SOUL

First Principle.—In order that perfect health may be realized and maintained in the human system, it is absolutely necessary that complete and continuous harmony be established among the three great factors in the human entity—body, mind and soul; and one of the first essentials to this end is the right use of these three factors in their respective fields of expression. The body must be used, under a circumstances, according to its true nature and real function; and the same is true with regard to the mind and soul; but it is not possible for any one of these three factors to be used as it should unless all three are used as they should. For this reason our purpose must not be confined to the right use of the body, or of the mind, or of the soul, exclusive of the others; but our purpose must be to find and continue the right use of all three in perfect harmony. There are many things that can be done to the end that this right use of body, mind and soul may be maintained; but the first essential is to inspire every element and force in the system with a strong, continuous desire to bring about this right use at once, and to the most perfect degree. In other words, we should resolve, from this moment on, to use the body, the mind and the soul according to their true nature; and we should make this resolution so strong that every part of body, mind and soul will *feel* the power of that resolution. The result will be that the entire system will respond more and more to what we have resolved to do, and in consequence we will develop within ourselves a second nature, so to speak, having a tendency to promote the right use of everything that exists within us. The law is, whatever you make up your mind to do that every power within you will help you to do; but your resolution must be strong and positive, and must continue to inspire every element within you all through life.

Second Principle.—Every element and force in the human body should be placed in action, at least to a certain extent, every day; and therefore, the great rule in physical culture is, to exercise daily every muscle in the body. The value of this rule becomes more and more evident the more perfectly we realize the fact that life can find expression only through those physical fibers that are exercised or that are given a certain amount of action every day; and in order to maintain health all through the system, the life force should be expressed continually through every part of the system. When a muscle remains dormant or unused for some time, it is weakened, and, in addition, may harden or ossify, and thereby originate old age conditions. Perfect health, however, demands perpetual youth all through the body; that is, perpetual renewal of all the elements all through the body, and also the full expression of life, vitality and virility through every fiber and cell. One of the first things, therefore, to do in this connection is to adopt a simple system of physical exercise that will insure the placing of every muscle into action at least for a few moments every day. To outline such a system of exercise will not be necessary here, as anyone can, through the use of a number of well-known exercises, ascertain what is necessary to place every muscle in motion every day. But these exercises when applied should never be strenuous, nor should they be carried out in a mechanical manner. The rule should be, when taking physical exercise, to try to combine the mind with the exercise, and expect results mentally, with full faith and enthusiasm. In other words, train the mind to enter into the exercise. You will thereby call into action the finer energies of the body as well as the purely physical energies; and this is exceedingly important, as a good, healthy body demands the full expression of all the forces of the personality, the finer nerve forces and vital forces, as well as the physical forces.

Third Principle.—In the right use of the body it is absolutely necessary that the life force be expressed and exercised in every cell and fiber of the body. No cell can be in good health unless it is absolutely filled every day and continually with the life force; and to this end, we should aim to secure a stronger and more complete expression of the life force throughout the physical personality. To proceed, concentrate your mind for a few moments upon the different parts of the body, and arouse at the time a strong desire for the full expression of the life force in every fiber and cell. In addition, try to picture or imagine the full expression of life in every part of your body, and enter into the exercise with the deepest depth of feeling that you can possibly realize at the time. This mode of concentration should be taken for a few moments several times every day; and if it is made strong, positive, deep and penetrating, the results will invariably be the increase of life and energy a through the physical system. Every cell will be made more active, every organ will perform its functions more perfectly, and there will be a decided increase in vitality, vital energy and working capacity. Besides this, a deeper realization of the life more abundant will be gained for the body; and we know full well, that the more life we feel in the body, the greater becomes the joy of living. This exercise, therefore, will accomplish many things, and should be entered into with earnestness and enthusiasm.

Fourth Principle.—The mind should be wholesome at all times and under all circumstances; and every form of wrong thinking should be eliminated completely. We cannot use the mind rightly unless every state of mind is wholesome, harmonious and constructive; and therefore no adverse mental state must be permitted at any time. To cultivate a wholesome mind the first essential is to train the mind to entertain harmony, purity, mental sunshine, positiveness, kindness, sympathy, loftiness of thought, aspiration, and the tendency to always look for the good and true and the beautiful in everybody and everything. The law is this, that it is practically impossible for ailments of any kind to enter the body so long as the mind is thoroughly wholesome; and, therefore, the cultivation of a wholesome mind becomes one of the great essentials in the attainment of perfect health.

Fifth Principle.—In the right use of the mind, it is necessary that we learn to think with the entire personality; that is, we should not simply think through the brain, but we should think through every nerve and fiber throughout the entire personal form; in fact, every cell in the system should act as a channel for the expression of mental power. To accomplish this, try to think of the entire personality whenever you use the mind in any way, or whenever you entertain a wholesome or constructive state of mind. In other words, whenever you think, or whenever you enjoy, invariably think of the entire personality, so that the enjoyment and the thought may, to a certain extent at least, enter into the personality and find expression through various parts of the personal form. In addition, take special moments every day for the purpose of training the mind to use the whole of the personal form as a channel for thought; and the exercise may be as follows: Take any quality such as health, life, power, personal worth, ability, or any quality desired, and turn your attention upon that quality with the deepest of interest. Then as you feel your mind entering into this quality with genuine interest, try to project the activity of the mind down through the personality; that is, try to extend mental action to every cell in your body. The mere effort to do this will produce results to a certain extent, and as the principle is practised, you will find that the mind will, more and more, extend its activities to different parts of the personality. Later you will discover that you can actually feel the action of thought in every fiber in your system; and it is then that you are really beginning to build up for yourself a powerful mind. No mind can become powerful so long as it uses the brain only; but when it begins to express itself through the entire brain, through all the nerve centers, through a the nerve fibers and through every physical cell in the system, as well as through every force in the personality, then the channels of expression for the mind will become so numerous and so extensive that all the latent forces and powers of the vast mental world will begin to come forth in greater and greater measure. The reason for this is evident, because when the mind can use the entire personality, the scope of mental action will increase to such an extent that the free and easy expression of every mental force may be promoted thoroughly and completely. This principle, in addition to the remarkable increase of mental power, will also establish greater harmony between mind and body, which is extremely important, because the mind cannot control the body so long as it finds expression only through the brain; but when the mind begins to express itself through the entire personality, then every part of the body will become more responsive to mental action, so that the complete mastery of the body by the mind may be realized; and the mind should exercise complete mastery over the body because in this way alone can the physical instrument be maintained in perfect condition under every circumstance.

Sixth Principle.—The mind should aim to fashion all thought in the image and likeness of the ideal. We do not use the mind properly unless we are always thinking towards the ideal; and the reason for this is found in the fact that we do not think the truth unless we are constantly aiming to enter into the realization of higher and greater truth; and to enter into the realization of higher and greater truth, we must think towards the ideal. The effect of this process upon health is readily discerned, because the mind will, when thinking towards the ideal, create more ideal and more perfect conditions in the mental world; and every condition that is created in the mental world will, sooner or later, find expression in the physical personality. The same practice of thinking towards the ideal will tend to perfect all the expressions of life through the mind or the body; and this is most important because it will tend to develop those finer states of life that are always wholesome and pure and in perfect harmony with the true order of the higher life within. To carry out this principle, we should select a number of the highest and best ideals that we can think of, and establish those ideals before the mental vision as clearly and distinctly as possible. Then we should frequently turn attention upon those ideals, and at every opportunity express a strong and intense desire for the mind to work up towards those ideals, or reach out for the higher realization of the truth and the life and the power that we know those ideals to possess. However, the application of this principle must be continued with faith, determination and enthusiasm. We must develop a passionate love for the ideal, and the entire system must become so filled with intense desires for the ideal that every fiber and atom will respond to the force of those desires. No effort must be half-hearted; but every effort must be whole-hearted. And as we proceed with the whole heart, we shall soon succeed in renewing the mind upon a higher plane of thought and life, and thereby transform the entire personality in the image and likeness of those higher and finer things that we are realizing in our growing consciousness of the ideal.

Seventh Principle.—The first essential in the right use of the soul is to think of the soul as the real you, as the real individuality, as the real self, and as the real and permanent master over everything in the human system. It is the soul alone that has the full light; it is the soul alone that has the full power to lead and to guide; therefore nothing can be right in mind and body unless it is inspired by the soul. It is the soul alone that knows what should be done or what can be done; therefore, the soul must occupy the throne. To apply this principle, we should train ourselves to think of the soul as the real self, and as the ruling power in everything we do; and we should also think of the soul as having the power to do everything right, and the wisdom to know what should be done at any time or under any circumstance. In the application of this principle, we will find that our consciousness will gradually rise more and more into the realization of the soul life; and as this higher realization is gained, we will begin to live in the soul instead of in the body where we previously lived. But our living in the soul will not weaken the body. On the contrary, the more fully we live in the soul the more life and power we will *express* both in mind and body; therefore, the result will be great gain in every possible manner. The law is this, that when we live in the higher, we become more able to provide everything necessary for the lower; and this is self-evident, because all life and power comes from the higher. When we learn to actually live in the soul we shall be able to gain possession of a far greater measure of life and power; and whatever we gain possession of in consciousness, that we invariably express throughout the personality. In addition to other gains that will be realized in this manner, we will find that the entire personality will be refined and made superior. But we must remember that this refining process in the personality will not make us more susceptible to the ills of life. It is the contrary that is true, for the fact is that the more refined and spiritual the personality becomes, the more immune the personality becomes from a weakness, from all ills, or from any adverse condition whatever. We shall find that the power of the spirit, when expressed in the body, can protect the body; and when this spiritual expression becomes strong; full and positive, the protection will become so complete that no ill can befall the personal form henceforth.

Eighth Principle.—The soul should be lived in every element and in every atom of the body. We should not simply be conscious of the soul, or conscious of the great truth that we are living in the soul; but we should *live* the life of the soul throughout our entire system; and then make that living so full, so strong and so thorough that we can actually feel the soul life in every part of mind and body. The soul is always pure, wholesome, harmonious and powerful; therefore, the more perfectly the soul is lived in mind and body, the greater will be the purity, the wholeness, the harmony and the power that we will realize in every part of mind and body. Perfect health must follow because when the pure, the strong, the perfect, the wholesome is expressed in every atom, there will not be room for discord, disease, weakness, or any adverse condition whatever. To apply this principle, proceed by training your consciousness to realize as fully as possible the existence of the soul life; in other words, try to become more and more conscious of the soul. Then enter so deeply into this consciousness of the soul that you can actually feel the life and the power of the soul. This feeling will gradually find expression throughout your personality; but you should increase this expression by creating a strong, positive desire for this expression, and by giving this desire added force and determination under every available opportunity. In brief, learn to *live* in the soul, and learn to give the soul life to every fiber in your being. This will mean the coming forth into the personality of that which is always we, always perfect, always wholesome, and always in peace, power and harmony.

Ninth Principle.—The conscious realization of the existence of body, mind and soul should be present to the fullest possible degree, in every thought, feeling and action; that is, whatever we do, we should always recognize all those three factors as being indispensable factors in every expression of life. The practice of recognizing body, mind and soul in everything we do, and the practice of giving fuller expression to body, mind and soul in everything we do will tend, first, to produce a larger and a more perfect manifestation of the elements, forces and powers that exist within us on a planes; and, second, to produce a more balanced and more harmonious state of relationship among these three great factors; and in health as we as in a desirable attainments, it is highly important that body, mind and soul harmonize, and also that the largest and best from the spiritual, the mental and the physical, find the fullest and most perfect expression possible. We should always make it a point to give *soul* to everything we do, and should always think of the soul as taking part in every action, whether of mind or body. We should always make it a point to combine mind and body in all life, in all enjoyment and in all functioning of the personality, whether physical or mental or both. Through this practice the three great factors—body, mind and soul—are trained more and more to work together in all the actions of life, and in all attainments and achievements we may have in view. And the greatest results must naturally follow where these three factors work together in harmony, and to the most perfect degree possible. Our aim should be to consider body, mind and soul in everything that we carry forward into expression, whether the plane of expression be physical, mental or spiritual.

Tenth Principle.—The soul is always perfect, and can be used as it should in life only when constantly recognized as perfect. Under a circumstances, therefore, we should think of the soul as being absolutely perfect in every form and manner. The mind grows more perfect as it grows more and more fully into the realization of the perfection of the soul. Therefore, we should encourage and prompt the mind to act more and more fully towards the perfection of the soul, because such action will invariably tend to develop the realization of perfection in every part of the mind. When the mind continues to ascend towards the marvelous, the wonderful and the sublime in the soul, every part of the mind will, accordingly, take on more and more of all that is high and lofty and perfect in the soul. The body, with all its conditions and states of expression, is invariably the direct effect of the present development and conscious realization of the mind. Therefore, when the mind ascends into the realization of the perfect, the complete, the higher and the better, the body will naturally respond, and will give expression to the higher and the better in all its functions and manifestations. In the attainment of health, we understand fully how the application of this principle must work wonders. In the first place, we realize that the soul is well; in the second place, the mind takes on the perfect health of the soul as the mind grows into the consciousness of the perfect health of the soul; and in the third place, the body becomes like the mind, therefore grows in the expression and manifestation of perfect health, as the mind grows in the consciousness of that perfect health that always exists in the soul. The application of this principle should receive our best attention, and should be entered into with unbounded faith and enthusiasm. This will mean a wonderful change for the better, which will finally culminate in complete emancipation.

CHAPTER XI.
THE FINER CURATIVE FORCES

Finer States of Mind.—Whenever the mind is in action certain forces are expressed, and if the mind is in a higher or finer state of action at the time, the forces expressed will be both finer and more powerful; and we realize that the finer energies of the mind have the power to exercise a far greater influence over the body, and, in fact, over the entire personality. Therefore, whenever we proceed to apply wholesome and constructive states of mind, we should try and make the actions of the mind as high, as fine, and as deep as possible; and one of the first essentials to this end is to become mentally serene—not only serene in a general sense, but become so perfectly still that you can actually feel the stillness of life and soul throughout your system. When the mind is in that state, it invariably gives expression to very fine energies. Those energies invariably have the power to penetrate a conditions of the system, to eliminate every condition that is not in harmony with perfect peace, perfect health and the perfect expression of true being.

There is a current belief that in order to change physical conditions, we must exercise a great deal of mental force; but this is not true; in fact, it is the reverse that is true. It is not a great deal of force that is necessary, but a deep, serene, highly refined state of mind, because such a state gives expression to those purer, more wholesome and more harmonious life currents that have the power to penetrate all through the system, healing, purifying, building up, harmonizing and making things right in every form and manner. And we realize that if these highly refined life currents could continue in expression all through the system, every day, for some time, all adversity would finally be eliminated, no matter what the conditions might be.

When we proceed to cultivate this conscious expression of the finer forces and the finer states of the mind, we build up a constructive process that will steadily take hold of the finer side of life, and will work through the interior currents, or the undercurrents, and gradually re-establish perfect health and perfect harmony throughout the deeper life of the system; and whenever the right is established in the deeper life of the system, the right will invariably manifest all through the external organs or form of the system.

Whenever we gain this finer understanding of life, our first object should be to train ourselves to enter into this higher, more refined and more serene state of the mind, and try to feel that we are actually reposing in that beautiful state—the state of perfect harmony, peace and wholeness, and, in fact, *resting there* in the full realization of the great truth that we are, in real being, always in perfect harmony and health. If we would continue in this state, we would find that we should not have to do anything else to regain perfect health, because that state of mind alone will gradually and steadily place in action all those higher and finer life currents—those life currents that invariably can and will restore order, harmony, health, wholeness and freedom to every part of mind and body.

The Finer Energies of Thought and Feeling.—One of the great laws to be considered in this important study is this, that whenever we actually feel perfectly well, regardless of physical conditions, we will begin to manifest perfect health from that very hour. The reason for this is found in the fact that feeling always goes beneath conditions and manifestations; that is, it goes down to the very root, so to speak, of all expressions of life, so that whenever we *feel* well in this deep, interior sense, we place in action a health producing life force at the very root, or at the very beginning, of all expressions and manifestations. The result, therefore, must be that all expressions and manifestations will become the way we feel, that is, wholesome, healthful and harmonious.

When we establish health, wholeness and harmony at the very beginning of all the manifestations of life—in the interior state of consciousness, we will naturally manifest health all through the system; and, therefore, we realize the immense importance of cultivating that deep, interior feeling of perfect health, that is, the power to *feel* well in the within at all times and under all circumstances. In this connection we must remember *that the way we feel inwardly, that is the way we become outwardly,* provided, of course, that this interior feeling is thorough and continuous along the line of feeling that we have chosen.

We all know that if we could feel young in this interior sense, and continually, instead of simply believing that we would like to be more youthful, the spirit of youth would be expressed all through the system, and we would gradually change the physical personality until it manifested the same condition of youth that we had continued to feel in the within. This is a law that cannot fail, and, therefore, we must not fail to apply it. It is true that the power to enter into this deep interior feeling, and *feel* the way we wish to feel, may involve much practice and concentrated action; but it is an attainment that we all can reach. And knowing that we invariably become in the without as we feel in the within, we should proceed toward this attainment with the greatest enthusiasm possible, and with the application of all the truth and information we have been able to gain on the subject.

To establish this deep feeling, we shall gain largely by realizing continually the great fact that we all are in the within perfectly well; that is, we should dwell on the great truth that the soul is always well; then we should proceed to enter into the feeling of that health and that wholeness that constitutes a permanent part of the soul life. When we know this truth, we know that our effort to *feel* perfectly well in the within is based upon a scientific principle, and that we are simply trying to feel what is absolutely and eternally true—that is, that we always are well in the within, and therefore we always should feel well in the within.

The Subconscious Forces.—There is no field of consciousness in the human mind that is so vast, and that contains such a large number of the finer life currents as the subconscious field; and, therefore, we realize that every effort that we may make to awaken the larger subconscious life will invariably result in the expression of a larger measure of life, especially the finer and higher states of life. In dealing with the subconscious we are dealing with a large subject, too large for detailed analysis in this connection; but in order to secure the best results in the simplest manner, we should realize that the subconscious mind will invariably respond to our conscious directions, and that whatever direction we may make to the subconscious, with a view of awakening the higher and the finer life currents from within, will be followed by response from within, at least to some measure; and as we learn to apply the law through which the conscious mind directs the subconscious for greater action, we will find that the finer life currents from within will express themselves more and more until the outer personality becomes literally charged with life and power from within—life and power of a very high and fine order. Every effort we make, therefore, in this connection will result in great gain both for the realization of perfect health and for the realization of greater personal power.

Spiritual Exaltation.—Among the many forces of life that may be found in the higher and finer states of consciousness, there are none that are finer or more powerful than those forces that are awakened and expressed when the mind enters what we may call spiritual exaltation; that is, when the mind is placed in an exalted state of consciousness. There are many experiences in the past as well as in the present, illustrating the fact that marvelous cures can be produced by what we term the exaltation of spirit. At certain times the mind is lifted and wonderfully exalted beyond material things, beyond anything in the objective—lifted up into another world, so to speak, where power is immense, where the light of truth is as brilliant as the shining sun, and where the consciousness of the perfect, the true and the absolute becomes an actual realization.

We know that faith invariably has a tendency to exalt the mind; and there are many lines of thought, such as worship in all its phases, that have the same tendency to lift the mind into the spirit. Besides this, there are many other tendencies that may come in daily life that tend to exalt the mind; and we shall find it profitable to employ any or all means that may have this tendency, although we can produce this remarkable exaltation in ourselves by turning our attention to the highest and purest state of spiritual being that we can imagine—then with all the power of life and mind and thought and soul, desire to realize the high spiritual state upon which attention has been directed.

When we proceed in this attitude, we will gradually turn all the energies of life upward, and those energies will begin to work toward the higher, rising continually in the scale of consciousness and lifting the entire mind upward into higher and finer states of being, until the state of glorious exaltation is realized. In many instances this exalted state is reached in a few moments of such consecrated effort; but under any circumstance, we can, through such consecrated effort, steadily and surely lift the mind more and more until the exalted state is realized absolutely; and when we do enter the exalted state, every adverse condition of the body disappears instantaneously. The reason why is this, that when consciousness is exalted, it enters into a world of pure spirit and marvelous power—a power that is perfect, whole, clean, healthful and thoroughly good in every way—a power that has the power to fill the entire being of man through and through and give expression to the pure, the wholesome, the harmonious and the perfect in every part of mind or personality.

In this connection we should also remember the great law that whatever we become conscious of, that we invariably manifest in mind and body; and, therefore, since we become conscious of this marvelous power when we enter spiritual exaltation, we invariably do, according to the law, give expression to that, power, and that power acts as a consuming fire, purifying the entire system and making every part of the system absolutely pure and whole. In brief, the power that we become conscious of through spiritual exaltation will express itself all through mind and body, pouring through the system like a powerful life current, or like a powerful refining current, removing all adversity and discord before it, and restoring absolute harmony and perfection to every part of the human entity.

Remarkable Possibilities.—If people who have distressing ailments and who have tried so many things without results, would proceed at once to train their minds to enter more and more into this state of exaltation, they would not continue very long in their present adverse condition. To proceed, they should turn attention upon the highest and finest state of being that can be realized and imagined, and then with the whole of life, that is, a yearning that is irresistible, and a desire that thrills every atom, try to realize this wonderful state of spiritual exaltation. If they would continue in this way faithfully, day after day, and week after week, if necessary, they would finally lift the mind out of the bondage in which they have been living, or would gradually rise more and more into the higher and finer, until some glorious day they would find themselves in the exalted state; and when this experience was realized, a marvelous change would come speedily.

Here we must remember that it is impossible for any ailment to continue in the body after the mind has been exalted in the spirit, because whenever that exaltation is realized, the entire system is literally flooded with new life, with new and highly refined forces, with new and wholesome states of being, with new and harmonious states of consciousness, with new and powerful states of mind; and in brief, complete renewal of the entire system is brought about, because the higher and finer powers from above have come down into the physical being, changing everything and bringing about a new order absolutely. The possibilities, therefore, that are within easy reach of everybody, in connection with what we term spiritual exaltation, are remarkable, indeed; and among a great means of healing there is no method that is more remarkable or more powerful than that of spiritual exaltation. It invariably means the absolute changing of everything, the lifting of life into the higher and the finer and the perfect, and the restoration of that perfect state of being that we know to be our inheritance from life—that perfect state of being that invariably finds expression all through the system when the power of the spirit is given full freedom in mind and body.

The Spiritualizing Process.—What we may term the spiritualizing process constitutes one of the most direct and one of the most effective means of cure that is known; and it consists, first, in realizing the power and the presence of the spirit in the system; and, second, in taking hold of the power consciously, and directing it wherever healing is desired. To illustrate, there may be a condition in your system that you wish to change, and your object will be to spiritualize that part of the body; or you will want that part of the body to undergo spiritualization, and you wish to apply the spiritualization process to that organ or function or part, whatever it may be. You proceed in this manner. You first realize the fact that you have conscious possession of certain spiritual forces—forces that are serene, harmonious, highly refined—pure white energies with healing on their wings. You realize that you have full conscious possession of those forces in your own being. You realize that you can direct them as you may desire, and cause those forces to act in any part of the body as you will. Thus you turn your attention to that part of the body that needs attention, and while concentrating there positively and with deep, calm feeling, you *think* that you are directing those spiritual forces all the way through that part of the body, causing those forces to move to and fro in that part of the body, literally penetrating every fiber and nerve, and entering into every atom, spiritualizing every element through and through in that part of the system. Briefly, that part of the body is being spiritualized by the moving to and fro of those fine, powerful life currents—currents that are purely spiritual and that invariably work for purity, harmony, health, wholeness and perfection of being.

Through this method you are not only establishing a spiritual process in that part of the body, but you are also giving expression to the higher and finer life currents that invariably find expression wherever the power of the spirit is directed. The result will be that you can almost see those finer spiritual forces with the eye of the spirit, gently but positively moving all through the atoms, elements, veins and fibers of your system, penetrating them all in this beautiful manner, giving powerful expression to this gentle, peaceful, harmonizing process. We repeat, you can almost see this wonderful, spiritual process taking place; and as you continue you will begin to feel that physical conditions are gradually losing their hold or dwindling away, or changing, or modifying, according to the powerful expressions of this deep, fine and health-producing force of the spirit. The undercurrents and the inner life, including the chemical actions of the body, are being acted upon, and are being influenced to change so as to harmonize perfectly with the true order of things. A greater power is in their presence, and therefore the lesser powers of the body will obey perfectly, and proceed at once to resume a state of order, harmony and health.

We realize that it is a very fine art to take hold of these wonderful spiritual life currents, direct them through consciousness, through the finer and more serene control of the will, and thus cause those higher forces to pass through and spiritualize any part of the body. And we should repeat frequently, until those finer forces, those pure white spiritual energies, gain complete mastery of the situation. For here we must remember that those spiritual forces always work for the good and the right and the true; and when they do secure mastery of the situation in any part of the body, the good and the right and the true will prevail in that part of the body. Emancipation will have been secured; health, life and power will have been restored, and all will be well again.

To train the mind to apply this process, we must develop a deep, serene state of mind, and try to enter more and more deeply into that perfect faith and perfect realization of the spirit wherein we absolutely know that we are in conscious touch with the powers of the spirit. Then we realize that we can direct those finer life currents and express them anywhere, just as readily as we can move the hand physically, or direct any part of the body; and wherever we may direct those highly refined spiritual forces, there those forces will proceed to act in a strong, positive and yet serene manner, always refining, always harmonizing, always healing, always restoring perfect order. They will spiritualize and make perfect; and wherever conditions are made perfect or spiritualized in any part of the human system, all ailments and all discord must instantaneously disappear. Results, however, will depend very largely upon our realization of the great truth that whenever we apply the spiritual process we are giving expression to higher power. We must be able to say to the body, "The greater is at hand." Then all physical conditions must obey absolutely and resume that higher, finer and more perfect state of being that is invariably produced by the presence and the power of the greater. We must also remember that there are no obstacles in the physical world to that power. That power can overcome any and every obstacle; and it always works for health, for peace, for harmony, and for the life more abundant.

CHAPTER XII.
LIVING IN THE ABSOLUTE

The Absolute State of Being.—When we speak of the absolute we have reference to that state of being that is changeless because it contains everything that life can hold; that is, everything that really is in life. The absolute is limitless and perfect in the extreme sense of those terms; and when we speak of the absolute, we refer to that state of perfection that has reached the climax, or where all perfecting processes have completed their work. However, we cannot conceive of any process as ever coming to an end, and yet there is one thing that we realize no matter how we may approach the subject, and that is, that everything that is to be perfected must first contain the possibility of perfection within itself.

We say that the soul will continue for all time to rise in the scale, ever becoming more perfect, meaning that the soul will continue to give expression to a larger and a larger measure of its own inherent life or divinity, its own inherent qualities and powers, all of which must be absolute—containing within themselves all that any quality can contain; in brief, we say that the soul in its growth and development continues to give expression to more and more of that which is inherent in the soul. But if the soul can continue to give expression to more and more of its inherent qualities, or its real spiritual life, and continue thus for an endless period of time, we must come to the conclusion that the soul already has within itself everything that can be expressed through an endless period of advancement and ascension.

The soul must necessarily have within itself absolute perfection if it can continue for all time to express more and more perfection; and we know that if the soul did not have within itself absolute perfection, it would in its development come to an end some time. However, if the soul never comes to an end in its process of development, but continues to rise in the scale for eternity, it must necessarily possess within itself at the present time the absolute state of being; and here let us remember that the absolute is without conditions, without limitations, and is not circumscribed in any way, but contains everything in the perfect, limitless state of real being.

The Unconditioned.—When we consider the absolute, we realize that we shall have to think quietly and deeply, because it is something that cannot be discerned unless we enter into the very spirit of Divine Wisdom; but we cannot enter into that spirit unless we are absolutely serene and the whole of life consecrated to the very highest we can think or know. When we enter into this deeper and more serene state of contemplation, we begin to understand what it means to live in the absolute.

As we approach that state, let us imagine an absolute state of being where the mind would be conscious of a perfection that could not be made more perfect, where the mind would be conscious of a life that was so beautiful that it could not be made more beautiful and where the mind was conscious of power and wisdom of all the qualities of the Divine—all that Divine Being could imply. In approaching such a state of consciousness, the first great truth that we would discover would be that there are no conditions in the absolute state, and there is nothing in that state that is undeveloped; in truth, in the absolute state all things are as they can be in the most extreme or highest form of being; but this is something that cannot be described in words. We can realize this only as we develop spiritual consciousness.

In contrast to this higher consciousness we find when we look upon our physical bodies, that the manifested side of life is full of changing conditions; and when we look upon the mind we find that there are degrees of manifestation and understanding; in brief, there are certain states that are constantly improving or in a process of perpetual growth. This is true of the entire personality, and is a part of the great plan; but in the absolute state there are no changes, no conditions, no growth, no advancement, because everything in the absolute state has reached the All in All.

Contains Everything.—When we consider this wonderful theme very closely, we find that, although the absolute state contains within itself everything that we can conceive of as existing in perfect being, still we must make a distinction between being perfect in the absolute, and manifesting perfection in the outer life; and in this connection there are three "views that we can take of the subject. The first view would be simply to consider the external side of life in a process of growth, and try, in the best manner we know, to improve upon that process continually through life. We would do this, however, without any regard to what we might possess in the within but in trying to grow or express ourselves without drawing upon the within, we would not accomplish very much. The reason for this is evident, because if we cannot secure the greater supply, we will necessarily continue in the same state of development all along until the greater supply is secured, which could only follow after we had placed ourselves in contact with the absolute life within.

We might take a second view, which would be to give no attention to external growth whatever, but simply live in the belief that we were perfect now, and, therefore, need give no further thought to external changes. In taking this view, our object would be to enter as deeply as possible into the consciousness of divine life, or realize the absolute state; and seemingly this would be the proper course to pursue; but there is another side to this great theme. The truth is that the mere act of becoming conscious of perfect being is not all there is in life. We must also consider manifestation. The fact that we are growing and constantly manifesting more and more in life proves that there is a purpose in such manifestation; and we know that the principle of that manifestation is this, that we do not really live, or cannot really live, without giving expression to more and more life. The giving of expression to more life involves the giving of expression to everything that pertains to life or that comes from life—all the powers, qualities and talents that exist in the human entity. Here we must also remember that it is not possible to manifest perfect being by simply working for the consciousness of perfect being. There are other essentials as we shall understand as we proceed.

The Higher Understanding.—Realizing then the great truth that growth, manifestation and expression are necessary factors in real living, we come to a third view of this subject; and that is, that our object in trying to live in the absolute should be for the purpose of manifesting a greater and a greater measure of the life of absolute being. Our purpose must not be to hide ourselves in absolute consciousness, or try to withdraw from manifested life, or in any way enter into that state of abstraction where we become more or less unconscious of things in the external. This must not be our object, although we know that it is possible at certain times to enter so completely into the abstract that we become in a measure oblivious to conditions. We find, however, that this state of obliviousness to conditions generally means that we have become insensible to them, and not that we have necessarily overcome them. However, while we are in that state we feel absolutely free from conditions; and a great many advanced minds have taken the view that real freedom can come only as we confine consciousness more and more to this abstract state where we become oblivious to the sensibilities of external life. But this is not the truth.

We know that, although we may live for a time in abstract consciousness, and in a measure realize freedom from pain and illness, still growth and manifestation will be taking place as usual in our external life. The body will continue its changes and the mind will continue to seek new forms of expression; natural processes will go on in the personality as before, and we shall soon find that the personality will require further attention. The fact is, we may isolate ourselves from personal conditions for a time, and it may be a delightful experience; and during that time, the personality may continue to run like a clock that has been wound up; but sooner or later the clock will run down, and the personality shall have to receive attention. In other words, the ego will be drawn out suddenly into manifested life to take care of its instrument. In the meantime, there may have been considerable loss sustained in the process of growth and development; and after all we shall find that there has been no real gain.

Dwelling in the Abstract.—There are many illustrations in history of this practice of the ego hiding itself, so to speak, in the abstract, and neglecting the personality; but in every instance, the personality either weakened or met with dissolution, so that there was no gain and much loss on the manifested side. True, there are advanced minds who argue that the personality is of no value in any case, and it matters not what happens to it so long as the soul finds absolute truth. But, whatever our view may be of that subject, we must come to the conclusion that the fact that we are here in this sphere of existence, in the possession of a personality, proves that our being here is for a purpose; and also that we have received this personality in order that we may use it as an instrument in fulfilling our purpose in this realm of existence. There may be times when it is well to enter the abstract for a short period, and thereby withdraw consciousness from the world of sense, but in most instances this is neither necessary nor desirable. It is not the highest light on this great subject; and it is the highest light that we all seek.

The Great Problem.—Considering the more rational view of this subject, that is, that the personality is necessary as an instrument of the soul, serving a great purpose, and that we should enter more and more into the consciousness of the absolute in order that we may further manifestation and growth in the personality, we are face to face with the great problem of adjusting ourselves to these two great phases of the truth. When we consider the external side, we find it undeveloped, and when we consider the spiritual side or the real I Am, we find that it is absolutely perfect, in need of neither growth nor further development. But we shall find the solution of this problem as we realize that growth in the personality depends more and more upon the deepening of consciousness in the absolute; and also that real living will increase or perfect itself only as we cause the perfect being in the I Am to manifest itself more and more in the outer life. You may enter into consciousness of the absolute, and you may discern that absolute being is changeless, perfect, beyond further growth, and yet the moment you become conscious of the absolute state you will realize that this state inherently demands continuous manifestation. In other words, the deeper you enter the absolute state, the greater becomes your desire to manifest more and more of the absolute in and through your external being.

Wonderful Truth.—The statement has been made that even though the Infinite is perfect, still the Infinite cannot be satisfied unless divine expression through the great family of human souls is made constant; and whatever we may think of this statement, it is most delightful to believe. It leads to the conclusion that we are just as necessary to the Infinite as the Infinite is to us. Infinite life, therefore, although inherently perfect, beyond a limitations, is not complete in its consciousness of life unless that life is manifested more and more through the countless souls of the cosmos. The more we think of this, the more reasonable it becomes, the more desirable it becomes and the more beautiful it becomes; and we find in the realization of this truth the very secret of secrets concerning the nearness between God and man.

The truth is that if we are just as necessary to God as God is to us, we have therein the real principle and the real need of divine unity. We all must admit that it is inconceivable to think of the family of human souls as being one with God if neither were necessary to the other; but the fact that they are all necessary to each other gives an eternal reason for endless unity between the

Infinite and every soul in existence. The same idea is applicable to the individual I Am and the manifested life of the personality. Our conclusion here must be that although the individual I Am is perfect in being, living in the absolute, still manifestation through the personality is absolutely necessary to the conscious existence of the I Am.

The I Am cannot live consciously without giving expression to life; and the giving of expression to life demands an instrument through which that expression can take place. If there were no manifestation the I Am would simply exist in a state of unconscious abstraction, and we can conceive of no reason why the I Am should exist at all if its existence simply meant eternal sleep in the absolute. We must have a reason for things; things must explain their existence or state of being in a satisfactory manner; and if anything exists at all there must be some cause for that existence. However, we can find no cause for an existence that would mean nothing more than isolation in an abstract state, or eternal sleep. We must accept, therefore, the other view, or rather the higher understanding of this great theme.

Absolute Consciousness.—When we take this other or higher view of absolute consciousness, and proceed to penetrate deeper and deeper into the marvelous state of absolute being, becoming conscious of more and more of the absolute in order that we may manifest the greater life of the absolute, thus expanding the mind, perfecting the personality and enlarging the life of the soul, we find not only a reasonable cause for a existence and all experience, but we discover before us a wonderful path—a path of endless existence and ascension too marvelous to even imagine. Beginning with this higher view of life, that is, that we grow and develop in the manifested life as we gain a deeper and a deeper consciousness of perfect being, we meet the great law that whatever we become conscious of, that we invariably express. Our purpose, therefore, must be to become conscious of a larger and a larger measure of the limitless life and the perfect life that already exists inherently in absolute being. And the more we become conscious of, the more we will manifest in the without, thereby making existence upon all planes richer, more wonderful and more ideal at every step of the endless way.

Health and Emancipation.—The problem in this connection is how to apply this principle to the attainment of health and emancipation. We know that in absolute being there can be no sickness or weakness or discord of any kind. There can be no such conditions, or any condition whatever in absolute consciousness; and the more deeply we penetrate absolute consciousness, the further we get away from a forms of conditions or limitations. The question then is, how we may, through the gaining of absolute consciousness, secure emancipation from adverse conditions. In this connection we must consider the great fact that whenever we become unconscious of weakness or sickness or discord those conditions disappear entirely from the personality. We will suppose that you have a pain in your body, and that you wish to become unconscious of that pain. But here let us remember that there is a difference between becoming unconscious of a pain and insensible to a pain, because we become insensible to a pain only when our nerves are deadened. Here, then, we find a marked difference. However, when we become unconscious of a pain, we do so by withdrawing consciousness from the field of action of that pain; and the fact is that those forces in your system that were producing the pain cannot act in that manner unless you continue to be conscious of the pain. You must be conscious of the pain in order that those forces can produce that pain, and when you cease to be conscious of that pain the forces in that part of the system can produce pain no longer. This may seem strange, but it is a strictly scientific fact. It is absolutely true to natural law, because mind and body are so closely related that the mind must give its consent to a process before that process can begin or continue anywhere in the physical system.

We will suppose again that there is discord in your system, and that it began through the violation of some law; you at once become conscious of that discord, and immediately your consciousness admits the existence of discord in that place—the existence of certain activities that can produce pain. Your consciousness continues to give its consent to those activities continuing in that mode of action that will sooner or later produce pain; and when the pain comes, consciousness immediately admits the existence of that pain, thereby giving those activities permission to continue in the producing of more pain. However, the very moment consciousness would refuse to grant further permission to those activities, and withdraw its presence from that part of the body, those activities would cease, and they would no longer produce pain. The fact is that whenever you withdraw consciousness from any field of activity in your physical system, those activities will subside or cease altogether; and therefore what those activities produced previously will not be produced any more; that is, the pain will cease to be, and nature will resume normal conditions. This is a law that we can reason out and prove for ourselves very readily, and we will soon be able to understand how no form of action can continue anywhere in the system unless we are conscious of it—unless consciousness is there permitting those conditions to continue.

The Great Secret.—The problem is to withdraw consciousness from any state of activity that we do not care to encourage; and there is where we find the consciousness of the absolute life to be indispensable. We know that we cannot cease the consciousness of the lesser until we gain consciousness of the greater; in other words, we cannot withdraw consciousness from a state of discord unless we can direct consciousness upon the opposite state—a state of harmony. And we can withdraw consciousness from any place only when we are able to direct consciousness to that which is the very reverse. In the personal life, however, we find a bundle of conditions, the very reverse of the absolute state. Therefore, if we wish to withdraw consciousness from those conditions, we must consecrate consciousness to the absolute state; that is, we must continue to approach the absolute so as to become more and more conscious of the absolute.

Understanding the Absolute.—To understand what it means to be in the absolute state, or even to imagine the existence of such a state, we shall find it necessary to give much thought to the very highest states of consciousness; and, although we may not always be able to form a perfect conception of the absolute state of perfect being, still we can form mental conceptions that are so similar to that state that they will give us, for the time being, an indication to how and where we should turn attention. And here we should remember that although we may become conscious of perfect being, that does not mean that we have become conscious of all there is in perfect being. Such a consciousness would require an eternity; but we can become conscious of perfect being; we can draw so near to the absolute state that we can form a clear conception of the life of the absolute. However, we can never become conscious of all that is in the absolute, because again, that would require an eternity. It is true that all who are spiritually awakened are conscious more or less of the absolute, and there are times when they can draw so near to perfect being that they can really feel that they are in reality the I AM. And here you should remember that whenever you can feel that you and the I AM are one and the same, then you are in absolute consciousness. However, you may continue to penetrate more and more deeply into that state for eternity, and the more deeply you penetrate into that state the larger the I AM becomes in your conscious understanding.

Art of Overcoming.—Resuming our consideration of the possibility of withdrawing consciousness from conditions by entering more and more deeply into absolute consciousness, we shall find that this practice will prove of exceptional value in daily life. The illustration given with regard to pain will hold elsewhere; and, in fact, there are a number of illustrations that could be mentioned. We will suppose further that there is a chronic ailment in your system; and if you know that the forces of nature are perpetuating that ailment simply because your own consciousness gives consent, you realize that you can overcome that condition and find emancipation by ceasing to give conscious consent to the perpetuation of that ailment. Here we find the chief secret of those who deny the existence of disease. They continue their denial until consciousness becomes more or less oblivious, both to the disease and to that part of the body. But it is not necessary to deny the existence of disease, although the method is more or less effective as it helps consciousness to get away from that form of confused activity, the fact being that when consciousness withdraws from any place in the system, it will no longer give cause to the discord or the disease that may be in action in that place; that is, the forces of nature can no longer proceed as before to reproduce that particular ailment. However, it is not necessary to deny the existence of disease in order to withdraw consciousness from the field of discordant activity. We shall find that the other method is far more effective; that is, the method of withdrawing consciousness from the world of conditions by consecrating consciousness upon the absolute. You realize, therefore, that if there is an ailment in your system you may secure emancipation from that ailment and overcome it and become unconscious of those activities by becoming more fully conscious of the absolute, which is unconditioned, and wherein all things are absolutely perfect, containing the All in All.

Image the True.—We shall find it an excellent practice to try to imagine the reality of the absolute state, and try to imagine that it is a state wherein there are no conditions—a state that involves the complete, the perfect, the All that is in Divine Being; and when we imagine such a state and try to direct consciousness upon that state, or try to combine our own present consciousness with the consciousness of that state, we shall find that in every instance our present consciousness will enter so deeply into the unconditioned state of the absolute that we become unconscious of conditions in the without. Thus consciousness will withdraw from the world of discord and confusion, and will no longer take part in the producing of ailment or pain; and here let us remember that when our own consciousness no longer takes part in the producing of ailment or pain, it is impossible for ailments or pain to continue another moment in mind or body. This indeed is a great truth, a most wonderful truth, and the more deeply conscious we become of the vastness and possibility of this truth, the sooner we shall realize complete emancipation, absolute health and all those higher and more beautiful states of being that we know we can find in the consciousness of the ideal. Our purpose, therefore, must be to enter more and more perfectly into the consciousness of the ideal, which is, in truth, the consciousness of absolute being—in absolute being every ideal is real; and when we have entered that state where we know and feel that every ideal is real, then indeed are we living in the spirit of the absolute—in the pure, white light of eternal truth.

www.ingramcontent.com/pod-product-compliance
Lightning Source LLC
Chambersburg PA
CBHW020431010526
44118CB00010B/523